Cross-Cultural Ministry

Cross-Cultural Ministry

Kevin T. Brown

Much MAHaLo.

To order additional copies of this book, contact:
Xlibris
1-888-795-4274
www.Xlibris.com
Orders@Xlibris.com
787848

Acknowledgments

There are so many people that have been instrumental in both the content and the contextual arguments presented in this book. Without them it would have been unlikely that this book would be have been published.

First I thank my Lord and Savior Jesus Christ, who taught me to love people in a way that I never could alone. I thank my Mother for her unrelenting faith in God, her life of prayer and the godly example she set in the early formation of faith in my life. I thank my wife "Minda" for her encouragement and understanding in writing this book. I thank the many pastors, ministers and church members who have been so instrumental in my walk of faith. God has used you to help me see the value of Cross-cultural ministries.

Contents

Introduction

Why should this book be written? This is a question many authors struggle with. Is it necessary? Is the topic important to people other than you? Pondering these issues could be quite discouraging, however in the search for one's purpose, one's reason for existence one must find courage to speak even when it seems to be little reason for our voice to be heard. In over 30 years of ministry, there has been one unchanging need in the life of people everywhere. This need is at the core of the work of the ministry. I say work because what we have been called to do is not easy. It will challenge not only our activity, the service we provide, but also our attitude about those to which we are to serve.

How do we feel about the poor and the rich? What is our attitude toward those who are not like us, socially or ethnically? What about those of a different belief or those that don't believe at all? Do we categories them or treat them differently? The work of ministry challenges all who answer the call by encouraging even commanding them to work across these boundaries. To be effective we much face our fears and reject the limitations that culture, ethnicity even religion can build in us. Cross-cultural ministry is the bridge that breaks the walls of separation. It is what makes the Gospel message available to all.

18 And Jesus came and spake unto them, saying, All power is given unto me in heaven and in earth. 19 Go ye

therefore, and teach all nations, baptizing them in the name of the Father, and of the Son, and of the Holy Ghost: 20 Teaching them to observe all things whatsoever I have commanded you: and, lo, I am with you alway, even unto the end of the world. Amen. (Matthew 28:18-20)

I have lived my life as an outsider looking into a culture seemingly foreign to me. As a young boy growing up in Atlanta, Georgia, I lived in a community largely made up of a single nationality or ethnic group. Even though the racial dynamics of our community was rarely the topic of discussion, there was a question as to why, in a city of over 400,000, didn't our community reflect the city's diversity. It was hard not to notice the lack of diversity in the neighborhood. Our community was largely one single ethnic group. This was considered normal.

> *"It was easy to make this normal behavior culturally also the norm for the church corporately."*

The church became a microcosm of the same paradigm. Churches in each community not only functioned under the norms of community, but in many ways celebrated their common likeness as unity. It was easy to make this normal behavior culturally also the norm for the church corporately. Building relationships based upon ethnicity is to be expected in society today, just as it was then. It is typical for people to build life within the construct of the community in which they live.

My life was everything but normal in this area. Somehow, I felt our drawn to people that were ethnically different from my community and church norm. I started traveling early in life. Even the High School I attended was in community different from my own. Traveling was something I really enjoyed. It allowed me to connect to people across the cultural and community norms associated with my community. I was motivated to know people beyond the physical appearance or cross-cultural distinctiveness. These encountered made me to realize how alike we are.

> *The real power of who you are will never be realizes until an outside connection is made.*

At the core people are just people. Race, ethnicity or culture norms may provide a basis for simple personal identity. The real power of who you are will never be realizes until an outside connection is made. These outside connections that determine the value of who you are and the overall purpose to which you were born. A focus on cultural and ethnic identity can promote blindness in areas of life. When the focus is on personal uniqueness alone it is difficult to see the bridges or connections we have to one another. It is that blindness, or at least failure to acknowledge these likenesses that give rise to racial/cultural bigotry and fear.

We were blessed to live in an extremely diverse city racially, ethnically and culturally. Why didn't our churches reflect the diversity around us? Even with Though there was a great diversity in our city, it was not reflected in the church. Even today, though quite a few years has passed, there still seems to be an inability or unwillingness to go beyond its boundaries of the norm. Back then churches would often come together and worship on special occasions, yet even then the community of churches would still reflect a similar demographic. We learned the safety of the familiar and was satisfied with it. Even among the familiar, I could not shake the great interest I had with diversity found beyond our norm. I did not know it then, but I now believe this was part of God's plan to help me understand the tremendous impact we could make if we were willing to stretch. People no matter their culture, ethnicity or social economic status are more alike than different. This is the foundation of Cross-cultural ministry.

Finding our true value

*7 For God hath not given us the spirit
of fear; but of power, and of love, and of
a sound mind. (2 Timothy 1:6-7)*

There is no fear in love; but perfect love cast
out fear: because fear is torment. He that feareth
is not made perfect in love (1 John 4:18)

> Fear is the enemy of our
> finding our true value

What is fear? Fear is a feeling whether based upon fact or fiction of an impending loss. Fear is also the foundational approach to knowing God. The Fear of the Lord is the beginning, the starting place for wisdom and knowledge. (Proverbs 1:7, 9:10). In Genesis 22 Abraham was tested and the Lord relegated his obedience to his fear of the Lord (Genesis 22:12). When we love God right it is easy for the world and others to see it as fear. Abraham was demonstrating his great love for God even above the love he had for his son. When we love God right it is easy for the world to see it as fear.

Growing up in church helped me to understand the basis of a love for God. It is an overarching feeling of awe surrounding our response to God. I learned that it was unwise to play with God. He was to be respected and the things connected to Him considered holy and worthy of honor or respect. My fear is that the progressive thoughts have so normalized God that He is no longer awesome.

> *When we love God right it is easy*
> *for the world to see it as fear.*

I remember being in a church after a communion service. The service was over but the elements used in communion were still on the table in front of the church. A young child came to the table and began to down the remaining cups of juice. I know that the child did not understand the significance of the ceremony, but within me I screamed "What are your doing?" Every fiber of my being saw the Lord's table as sacred. This attitude was instilled very early in my life. Was this fear, legalism, or was this a display of man's love for a Holy God?

There is a difference in fear and being afraid. Fear is the since of awe and reverence that should always be connected to our experience with God. In the Hebrew Bible, (Old Testament) man's response to God was always associated with fear. When God presented himself to Israel, on Mount Sinai, His presence first created an atmosphere of fear and Israel stated as much saying to Moses "Speak thou with us, and we will hear: but let not God speak with us, lest we die." Their being afraid, kept them from approaching God. How can one man's fear draw him close to God and help him know and understand him, while another man's fear cause just the opposite effect?

> **"There is a difference in fear and being afraid."**

There is a connection between fear and love. The fear of the Lord was connected to the law of God. His legal standard clearly reveals the heart of mankind. Paul said the the law was given that every mouth would be stopped and that all would be guilty before God.

On a trip to Nigeria I was overwhelmed with the amount of religious activity that permeated the city. There were churches everywhere and many church conferences taking place. The many color billboards, advertisements and general acceptance of religious jargon in the public arena was embedded in the culture. We saw signs stating, "God is Here!" Even politicians placed on campaign vehicles "God's Team". Yet with all the religious slogans there seems to be a disconnect between these declarations and the overall societal norms. I find the same type of saturation in the USA. I attended a Promise keepers meeting years ago in the Alamo Dome in San Antonio, Texas, where 60,000 men from across the country gathered to worship God. On the drive home, the news of the moral decline in our country made me wonder, how so many men could be committed to the Lord and immorality, bigotry and lawlessness plagues our country. The problem with normalizing God in society is the subtle loss of the since

> **"We must never allow familiarity to take away our sense of "awe" toward God."**

3

of awe in our understanding of God. Familiarity has bred contempt and there is no more fear of God. We must never allow familiarity to take away our sense of "awe" toward God. We can easily relegate natural disasters, hurricanes, fires and floods to be acts of God. This feeds into the feeling of fear in the sense of being afraid without connecting it to God's deep love for us. To know God is our deepest pursuit. To understand his love our greatest reward. When we love God right it is easy for the world to see it as fear. We serve, worship and follow God even while facing personal loss or discomfort. This doesn't make sense in a world that is self-centered and self-preserving. What I am saying is the fear or reverence for God is the starting point to approaching Him.

Everyone, in some way, has something in which they value. Things we value can be physical, social or even psychological. Fear is connected to the value we place on potential loss. There are three areas of potential loss in life. There is positional loss, power loss and personal loss.

Positional loss could be a job or promotion. It could be family relationships or friendships. Positional losses are extremely challenging because the effect the perception of our identity. Firing from a job feels like a personal attack not a professional act. Remember everything we have positionally is temporary. This is the reason Christ said to not put your treasure in earthly things.

> Jesus taught about power as authority revealed and released in serving not being serve.

A loss of power deals with our ability to influence others. We all like to feel as if we are in control. Control is an illusion. True control must be able to account for every variable. Jesus taught about power as authority revealed and released in serving not being serve.

Personal loss deals with relationships. This type of loss can have lasting effects on a person's life. Lamentations 3 speaks of a man that experienced personal loss. He found his strength is the known mercy of the Lord. "It is of the Lord's mercies that we are not consumed…." (Lamentations 3:22)

The Great Commission

19 Go ye therefore, and teach all nations, baptizing them in the name of the Father, and of the Son, and of the Holy Ghost: (Matthew 28:19)

Jesus would commission his disciples to go and disciple nations. What a huge undertaking for anyone. The challenges would be enormous. Even today we face challenges to the work and message of the gospel. They include money, messaging and methodology. How would the work be financed? How do we keep the messaged central, among the ethnic and cultural barriers in existence beyond what we know as normal? How do we bridge the cultural divide to share what has been revealed? I am certain that these were issues of their day as well. The answer is simple, we must change. To take the Gospel beyond what we see as normal, we must change. This is the essence of cross-cultural ministry. Jesus took people from a very closed religious society and commissioned them to change the world while knowing the process would also impact their own life.

Jesus took people from a very closed religious society and commissioned them to change the world...

The Great Commission would not only bring the greatest message of God's grace to a world indifferent to him, it would radically change those commissioned to bring that message. In going they would not only change the world, they too would change. They would have to break from the religious and social norms and become cross-cultural in their missional efforts. Paul would become all things to all men to gain some. Peter would gain fresh perspective on God's perception of all mankind. Now the lines between acceptable norms were being eliminated. The gospel message did something the law or cultural standards did not. The gospel made no distinction between people or people groups. The gospel saw all of mankind as sinners in need of the saving grace found only in Jesus Christ. Paul summed it up by saying "If Christ died for all then all were dead". The gospel was not limited to any single group of people. It would embody the extended grace of God given to all men. That grace was solidified by the sacrifice Jesus made on the cross. This was God's love demonstrated.

> The gospel was not limited to any single group of people.

Cross-cultural Ministry

Behold, Thou shalt call a nation that thou knowest not, and nations that knew not thee shall run unto thee Because of the Lord thy God and for the Holy One of Israel; for he has glorified thee. (Isaiah 55:5)

Cross-cultural ministry are efforts made to declare the gospel beyond the familiar. It is a wholistic view of the great commission and its effects on both the receiver and the sender. The emphatic declaration of The Prophet Isaiah doesn't say the call to missions is optional. He declares "You shall call a nation…". His description lays the foundation for the missional mindset. He describes that nation as unfamiliar. It would be a people unknown to you, nor will you be known to them. Yet there will be a compelling element that draws you together. The only shared connection would be recognition of the touch of God upon your life.

...the call to missions is optional...

God has places something significantly attractive within those that are willing to answer the call. While it would be difficult to see this significance, God would allow it to be seen by others. It is easy to personally devalue what God has done in our lives. As we share the message of the hope we have in God, the Gospel message become clear in the mind of the hearer. There response to the message impacts and transforms our lives. It is amazing to be used by God. It is even more amazing and humbling that God would choose to use us for such an important task.

Paul recognized the power of the gospel. He called it the power of God to everyone that believes. (Romans 1:16) This is the impact on those that receive. In Judaism a great amount of effort was made to distinguish themselves from the world around them. Now they were commissioned to carry the Gospel beyond what they considered normal to other nations, even those outside of Judaism. They would have to see the world differently. It would be no more distinctions between Jew and the Gentile, bondman or free, male or female all would be one in Christ.

I was in a meeting of church leaders and one of the leaders said something that ignited a fire in my belly. On the surface it sounded like a rational statement. This is what was said "Even though they are different from us... We still love them." When I heard this, my heart melted, and I was overwhelmed, I thought if we see the world as different from us it is easy to build walls that keep us from each other, a wall is place between us. This wall almost gives us permission to fail in reaching the lost because we are so different. The "us verse them" mentality is a wall that limits the believer's effectiveness in reaching the world. In fact, Paul's writing reveals the distinction between the believer and the world is differentiated only by an experience with God through Jesus Christ.

"Even though they are different from us…

9

Rotten Apples

1 Corinthians 15:50 Now this I say, brethren, that flesh and blood cannot inherit the kingdom of God; neither doth corruption inherit incorruption.

The imagery speaks of the natural processes in a world marked by sin. The consequences of sin is death. The word death literally means separation. When sin entered the world, it brought separation. In the life of mankind this effected all relationships, with God, with man, and with the earth itself. The relationship with God, that brought life became a reminder of the disappointment brought about by sin activity. From this point death reign. Now we and everything around us is in a state of decay. At best, mankind works hard to simply delay the decay.

> In this world, nothing goes from bad to good without outside intervention.

In this world, nothing goes from bad to good without outside intervention. This reality makes it difficult to fix broken relationships. Like rotten apples, when relationship break, when people are hurt, it is easier to permeate the brokenness than to endure the discomfort leading to true healing. Rotten apples make an impact on fresh ones. It doesn't cause fresh apples to go bad because they are already in a state of decay. It does provide permission for the decay to advance. Only divine intervention can heal a hearting heart. Christ came heal broken hearts and pay the ultimate price for sin.

Know ye not that the unrighteous shall not inherit the kingdom of God?... (1 Corinthians 6:9)

And such were some of you: but ye are washed, but ye are sanctified, but ye are justified in the name of the Lord Jesus, and by the Spirit of our God. (1 Corinthians 6:11)

There has always been a desire for distinction when looking at religion in general. This is also especially true in the contrast between believers and non-believers. The scripture reveals a truth that even the Jews did not want to embrace about their relationship with Gentiles (Non-Jewish people). We are more alike than we may wish to think. Even if we grew up in a Christian home and kept all the traditions of the church, we must never forget the effect of sin upon all humanity. This includes those that are outside the walls of our churches as well as those inside. All have sinned and come short of the glory of God (Romans 3:23)

Salvation was not just behavior modification

Salvation was not just behavior modification. It was not about making bad people good. Our condition was far worse. A young person asked me one day "Pastor don't you have to do something really bad to go to hell?" I thought about is a moment, not wanting to provide impulsive answer and said "In reality, you don't have to do anything to go to hell… But if you want to go to heaven you will have to do something. A person must repent of your sin, Confess Jesus Christ as Lord and Follow and obey Him." Many people just want to live their life feeling they are ok because they haven't done anything, really, bad. Yet find they have no relationship with God. There will be a lot of good people in hell, just like there are a lot of good people in the world, at least by the world's definition. This is what the Apostle Paul wrote "For the love of Christ constraineth us; because we thus judge, that if one man died for all, then were all dead." So, salvation is not given to make bad people good, it is to make dead people live.

A Likeness Paradigm

We will never be effective until we can see beyond the surface. It is within the confines of a likeness paradigm that Jesus speaks to his twelve disciples the words of the great commission. "Go ye therefore, and teach all nations... (Matthew 28:19)

> Cultural Identity represented by kingdoms, languages and culture would not be abandoned.

(God) ...hath made of one blood all nations of men to dwell on all the face of the earth, and hath determined the times before appointed, and the bounds of their Habitations; (Acts 17:26)

There is neither Jew nor Greek, there us neither bond nor free, there I neither male nor female: for yea are all one in Christ Jesus. (Galatians 3:28)

What did this mean? Was God in fact getting rid of the cultural identity of the nations? The short answer is no for if he was eliminating cultural identity how could John speak of a multitude from all nations and kindred before the lamb of God. He wrote "After this I beheld, and lo, a great multitude, which no man could number, of all nations, and kindreds, and people, an tongues, stood before the throne, and before the Lamb, clothed with white robes, and palms in their hands;" When he asked who they were, the Lord replied "... These are they which came out of great tribulation, and have washed their robes, and made them white in the blood of the Lamb." He simply stated that all nations, all languages, and even all people will be in this congregation. Cultural Identity represented by kingdoms, languages and culture would not be abandoned. In fact, those things which define us would be redeemed. It is at that time when Revelations 11:15 will come to past saying, "The kingdoms of this world are become the kingdoms of our Lord and of his Christ; and he shall reign for ever and ever."

Created for a Higher purpose

Go into all the world and preach the gospel to every creature. Mark 16:15

Marks record of the great commission come on the heels of what may the greatest failure of a follower of Christ. His closest friends had completely ignored the observed power Had shown them in His short three and a half years of ministry. You would have expected them to trust what he had told them while he was with them. He taught them about the kingdom ruled by God. He should them God's absolute authority over sin and even death. Yet the horrific events that proceeded this moment could not be ignored. That witness their master and friend brutally beaten and killed on the cross. It was the worst type of death imaginable.

Christianity is based upon a realization we have been created for a purpose greater than our personal comfort or convenience

Christianity is based upon a realization we have been created for a purpose greater than our personal comfort or convenience. In it we were taught the importance of giving. It was normal to give money, time and talent to the church. Why was giving so important? While churches and ministries function largely through the voluntary donations receives, this only represents only one part of the overall purpose of giving. Giving is the heartbeat of God. John 3:16 said "For God so loved the world, "he gave." God's sacrifice was our example. The sacrifice made by Jesus Christ was an act of both submission and obedience to the Father.

We learned to serve, to work for what we wanted. In fact, most of what I understood about the church centered around sacrifice with a goal of somehow succeeding in life, yet not much changed. Church was very central to our life with multiple services on Sunday and almost every night of the week. We attended church on a regular basis. It was the most valuable use of our time. As a young boy it was just normal. Services could last for hours even on school days. Some night services would carry over until the next day. Long hours and frequent services became the norm of our life. There were no excuses. There was nothing more important not even school. We just got up and when to school with no excuses and no complaints. On top of this my mother sang in a high in demand coral group. She traveled as a member of a singing group and so did we.

> The culture of balance has become a breeding ground for division and separation.

Today, follows of Jesus Christ live to find a balance between commitments between spiritual things and natural things. There is a great sensitivity to time. The reasoning seemed sound and reasonable. Yet in our balanced culture today, violence is on the rise, hatred, bigotry and racism abounds. The culture of balance has become a breeding ground for division and separation. Sadly, the church has fell prey to this same cultural norm. We have become recipients of what I term the Samson Spirit. We have received a haircut, we look good, but we have lost our power. The realization of this loss was not known until he was faced with the enemy. The same is true with the church who lives in the illusion of power until it is tested and find the power is gone. We say the right words, pray the right prayers and sing the right songs. We have perfected the process of presentation with great precision and creative expression, yet our impact is without power. This results in a church more submitted to the culture than to Christ.

In the church there was an expectation of God's power. Their commitment to God was evident in their daily life and family. They believe their commitment to God would impact their lives and local community. There was little consideration given to the impact of church on the world. Though we did a lot at the church there was still something missing. It was the quest for purpose beyond the walls of the church and its local community.

Not all churches are the same.

There are two basic constructs of church in my life. There is the suffering church and the conquering church. The first is like the Noah model, where one preacher spent one hundred and twenty years building in response to Gods command. He suffered through ridicule, and never compromised his mandate from God. When the doors of his lifelong sacrifice closed, only he and his family

He obeyed and sacrificed, giving up everything considered normal in his life to save only his family...

remained. He obeyed and sacrificed, giving up everything considered normal in his life to save only his family. Today this would be considered ineffective ministry. Through this story Noah would be given a covenant with God and a place in the hall of fame of faith.

By faith Noah, being warned of God of things not seen as yet, moved with fear, prepared an ark to the saving of his house; by the which he condemned the world, and became heir of the righteousness which is by faith. (Hebrews 11:7)

The conquering church is more a Joshua model. At the time of Joshua's rise to leadership, he was well respected, and easy for the people to follow. His spirit was alive unto God. God would use him to not only lead Israel in to the promise land but to systematically inherit the land promised to them by God. There were few tears with this group. Their complete focus was to claim the inheritance.

Moses my servant is dead; now therefore arise, go over this Jordan, thou, and all this people, unto the land which I do give to them, even to the children of Israel. (Joshua 1:2)

And they answered Joshua, saying, All that thou commandest us we will do, and whithersoever thou sendest us, we will go. According as we hearkened unto Moses in all things, so will we hearken unto thee: only the Lord thy God be with thee, as he was with Moses. (Joshua 1:16-17)

Both models were and continue to be necessary today for God's divine plans to be revealed. One model was designed to preserve life the other designed to advance in life. Both remind us of the importance of both sacrifice and courage we need on this journey. If there is a balance to be sought it is the one concerning the sacrificing and conquering church.

I was playing golf with a young man recently. He was a very good golfer who loved the game. His plan was to one day be a professional golfer. When he came to Christ, he gave up the idea. This was his sacrifice to follow Christ. He gave up his dream to make himself more acceptable to him. Our acceptance by him is not contingent of our sacrifice. At best, our sacrifice makes us feel more deserving of his acceptance. In the parable of the talents, the Lord call the the servant which buried his gift wicked. The servant's reason for burying his gift was his impression of his master.

> At best, our sacrifice makes us feel more deserving of his acceptance.

Matthew 25:24 ... "I knew thee that though art a hard man, reaping where thou hast not sown, and gathering where thou had not strawed:"

To him, his Lord wasn't the giver of the talent, he was a taker. The passage also reveals an attitude of bitterness toward God. He didn't see him has just. God did not see the suppression of his as a benefit. In verse 30 he called him an unprofitable servant. His punishment was great for this oversight. In this passage honor was for the person using his talent. They were blessed and received not only multiplication but increase. The investment of his talent brought not only multiplication but addition for God added more to what he had. We will never be fully justified by our sacrifice. We are justified by His sacrifice alone.

Forasmuch as ye know that ye were not redeemed with corruptible things, as silver and gold, from your vain conversation received by tradition from your fathers; But with the precious blood of Christ, as of a lamb without blemish and without spot: Who verily was foreordained before the foundation of the world, but was manifest in these last times for you, Who by him do believe in God, that raised him up from the dead, and gave him glory; that your faith and hope might be in God. (1 Peter 1:18-21)

Sacrifice or Obedience

A sacrifice is simply a substitute for obedience. Obedience to God is an expression of our love for Him.

Genesis 22:12 And he (the angel) said, Lay not thine hand upon the lad, neither do thou any thing unto him: for now I know that thou fearest God, seeing though has not withheld thy son, thine only son from me.

Reverence is both love and fear...

The word fear is and interesting choice of word. It expresses an observation of his actions from a perspective of another. What Abraham did was an expression of love from his perspective. From the perspective of others, it is overkill, more than necessary. Reverence is both love and fear because what is an expression of love on our part can only be describe as fear to others. Fear is an emotional response based upon a perception of loss or harm. Yet fear is used to describe the foundational relationship between God and man or better said man to God.

The word God indicates the worship or reverent acknowledgement of an entity processing supernatural power. The reverent nature of this relationship is a recognition of authority to the point of willing submission. This relationship sees submission as the only option for failure to do so would be considered foolish.

Proverbs 1:7 The fear of the Lord is the beginning of knowledge, but fools despise wisdom and instruction.

Psalms 14:1 The fool said in his heart, "There is no God."...

God test the heart of his people through a clear understanding of loss of more than stuff. It is the loss of relationship with Him. His story, the story of God, is an explanation of man's connection to Him. It is not man's pursuit of God, but the recognition of the connection God has already established with man. The foolish heart seeks to undo this established and continual connection. Denial of the facts do not change the facts. Denial of the facts only make the one in denial foolish in his thoughts. Anyone in cross cultural ministry must be incredibly sensitive to the connection God has made in every man regardless of tradition, culture or even religious practices. The connection between man and God also binds mankind together. God has shown himself in every nation and culture in a way familiar to them. We must identify and provide evidence of his fact. It is not our mission to tell them something new but tell them something good. We are to tell them the Kingdom of heaven is at hand. We are to tell them the God of all creation has come to them. Our mission is not to provide information but explanation.

The church's teaching on sanctification and sacrifice was deeply rooted in making the believer's love visible to the world. Through this a strong reverence for God was formed in my understanding of God and his will for our life. Yet while we focused on sacrificed, other church models added the conquest paradigm to their normal. They believed in the life of abundance supply. By design both abundance and sacrifice must coexist in our understanding of God. The only way to fulfill the great Commission is to through both sacrifice and supply.

The Supply Side

While some churches build through sacrifice others build through supply. A speaker told a story of two groups of people. They both wanted to do something about hunger in their community. One group called for a fast to raise awareness of this situation. Many people joined with them in their movement and received much publicity in the process. The other group planned a banquet and charged $100.00 a plate for their hunger project. They invited many people in their city to attend and raise a tremendous amount of money to help purchase food for those in need. Which model was more effective?

> Much of what we do in church is based upon our perception of the purpose and mission of the church.

Much of what we do in church is based upon our perception of the purpose and mission of the church. Within some church models, the most effective use of their time an energy is to raise awareness of issues while others take a more active role in social change. There is no right or wrong way to do what is right. Knowing what God has called the church to do becomes the measuring rod of ministry activity. It doesn't matter, the means by which we do things, we all have been given an assignment by God. It is called the Great Commission.

The Great Commission

Go ye therefore, and teach all nations, baptizing them in the name of the Father, and of the Son, and of the Holy Ghost: Teaching them to observe all things whatsoever I have commanded you: and, lo, I am with you alway, even unto the end of the world. Amen. (Matthew 28:19-20)

And he said unto them, Go ye into all the world, and preach the gospel to every creature. (Mark 16:15)

The last words to the follows of Christ was to "Go into all the world and preach the Gospel'. Have you ever wondered why he did this? First let me state the obvious. God sent them to declare the message of them Gospel. This mandate indicates a need for the gospel to be heard. This is a tremendous change from the theology of the Old Testament.

> Is the great commission only to get the word out to the lost?

Is the great commission only to get the word out to the lost? Could there be another reason for the church to share this good news. I believe something happens not only in the life of the person receiving the gospel but in the life for the person answering the call to go. In my early years in church there were a group in our church called missionaries. They were typically women serving as teachers. They dressed in white, covered their heads with hats or handkerchiefs. They were modest and godly influencers in the church. Functionally, I never knew what they did as missionaries.

A few years ago, I heard a missionary speak about his experience in Brazil. Now, I had heard many missionaries share before, but this was different. Most of the mission's stories speaks of the things the missionary or

> We learned the safety of the familiar and was satisfied with it.

team did to help a community different from their norm. They speak of building churches, schools and digging wells then they ask for support to help them continue the work. Some even challenge us to engage in efforts to stop human trafficking, to help starving children, stop abortion or encourage adoption. Horrifying stories of the hunger starvation and unsanitary conditions grip our hearts and moves us to a compassionate response to the human need. Yet in this story, I heard about a man on a mission to impact a people group different from his own was personally impacted by his experience with them. Though he was the teacher he was being taught. The story he told was about a spiritual people. Though they were spiritual there was a limited understanding of the source of their spiritual connection. Like Phillip with the Ethiopian Eunuch, He started where he was to introduce him to Christ. We too must start where people are to reach them in cross cultural ministry.

Cross-Cultural ministry is not cultic or systematic brainwashing. It is helping people see, hear and understand the Lord's work in their life. God is not waiting on us to show the world who He is. He has given us his Spirit to help

> Cross-Cultural ministry is not cultic or systematic brainwashing.

us identify his work in the lives of all people to help them believe. In every culture the reality of God is apparent. What is unknown is his great love he has for all people. Consider the Apostle Paul as he speaks on Mars hill: He saw what they did as very religious to worship so many things. He noticed among all the god's they worshipped way one with the inscription "TO THE UNKNOWN GOD". After all their creativity in trying to make a god or deity for everything, they recognized their limited understanding of God. What did Paul do? He used this inner longing for knowing god as an opportunity to reveal the truth of who God is. God used their creativity to reveal who he was. He started where they were. To minister cross culturally we too must start where people are. Just as Paul did, we must show God's handprint upon all people. Cultural investigation will reveal God's handiwork.

The Heavens declare the glory of the Lord.

God uses everything to declare who he is. In this passage, the psalmist revelation of who God is is revealed in what God has created. God exist apart from created things. The reality of God the creator is revealed in the things created. The lordship of Christ is declared by His revealed greatness and power. The revelation of God in the heavens and the earth is also shown in all mankind. Before we can minister to people, we must first recognize their true value. They are not different from us. Their experiences, culture and culture may be. Everyone needs to know God. The essence of who God is only revealed in Christ.

> Before we can minister to people, we must first recognize their true value.

At the basis of cross-cultural ministry is not reaching different people. It is about serving people in behalf of God. I claim no real expertise in doing this, however, I have just made some observations in this process.

In over 30 years of ministry, I have seen first hand the importance of serving God's people. God's people are not limited to geography, culture or ethnicity. In fact, what makes the body of Christ unique is the inclusive nature of it. It is a place where people of every nation, tribe and tongue can come together, thrive, support and serve one another. Our ability and willingness to serve the body of Christ is the test of our identity. The biblical term use in the scripture is "love". Love is not limited to a feeling or emotion, it is the result of a conscious decision to commit to a person or cause more important than our personal comfort or even life. This is the nature and life of a servant and it is into this grace that we are called.

We are called to be a servant one too another. Being a servant doesn't seem like anything to aspire toward, yet to God it is the highest position of grace. Christ told his disciples that the one that would be the greatest must become the servant of all. The call to servanthood is the highest calling in the life of a Christian. So how do we serve? Is it out of good gifting or need?

> Christ told his disciples that the one that would be the greatest must become the servant of all.

Some would argue that we should only serve in an area of our gifting. While it is true that being gifted in an area would make serving easier and possibly even more fruitful, it is not the mantle of a servant. With a servant, calling is greater than gifting. The Bible is filled with individuals that were not gifted for a given task. Moses provided a convincing argument why he was inadequate for the task. God only reminded him that he was created by him and knew more about his capacity that Moses did. With each reason/excuse God had an answer. Today it is no different. It is easy for people not to recognize the work of God in them. Moses was the perfect candidate for the work though he did not see it. With him cross cultural ministry was going to his own people. He knew the ways of Egypt. He understood the protocol of the house of Pharaoh. Speaking to Israel was another matter. God never equipped him to do this but provided a resource, Aaron, through which this would be done.

The Old and The New

And the Lord God commanded the man, saying, Of every tree of the garden thou mayest freely eat: But of the tree of the knowledge of good and evil, thou shalt not eat of it: for in the day that thou eatest thereof thou shalt surely die. (Genesis 2:16-17).

The overarching dialogue of the Old Testament was an examination of the effect of sin in the world. Sin changed everything. It affected man's relationship to God, fellow man and all of creation. Sin truly brought death into the world. What is death? It is defined as the cessation (ending) of life. Death is not possible unless life was present. Sin brought death. Death is separation. This is the paradigm of the Old Testament. Separation effectively kept people distant from one another and distant from God.

> Separation effectively kept people distant from one another and distant from God.

Salvation was designed for life. Life is the opposite of death. If death is separation life is bringing things together. There is nothing more powerful that unity.

Psalms 133:1 Behold how good and how pleasant for brothers to dwell together in unity.

Psalms 133:3 ....For there the Lord commands a blessing even life forevermore.

Unity is the birthing place of life. It was when 120 disciples were with one accord, in one place where the church was born. The survival of the church is vested in its unity.

Jesus said that a house that is divided against itself cannot stand.

Paul said I beseech you brethren by the Lord Jesus Christ, that you all speak the same thing and be of the same mind and the same judgment. 1 Corinthians 1:10

Both admonishments speak of the importance of unity. The Lord himself recognized the power of unity. He gives us one mission "Go into all the Word" to declare "One Lord, One Faith and One baptism." The purpose of ministry gifts is the unity of Spirit in the bond of peace.

Endeavoring to keep the unity of the Spirit in the bond of peace. Ephesians 4:3

Did God know we were different? Yes, He did. He created us and knows the distinction that

> God made us in diversity not to separate us but to lay the foundation for new life

his has place in each of us. From the beginning, He created man and woman different. This difference was not meant to as a point of contention or division. It was a complimentary distinction design for unity with the purpose to bring life. It took the two becoming one before life could exist. In the same way it will take a believing people coming together for life to come in the place of our distinction.

God made us in diversity not to separate us but to lay the foundation for new life. Distinction creates an opportunity for unity. Unity is the foundation for life to exist. The church was designed as a place of diversity. In Acts 2 people from diverse background and languages came together in unity and the church was born. God commands life in the place of unity and only unity. The purpose of cross-cultural ministry is not the recognition of diversity but the promotion of unity. Jesus' prayer was not for God to make us special or unique but to make us one. Jesus' desire was for the church to understand and embody the same type of unity He has with the Father.

In the Garden

Before sin, his wife found her complete identity is her husband. She did not complain about it or see him as demanding or domineering. There is nothing in scripture indicating a distinction between the two, Adam and his woman. When God called Adam, his wife was to present. Even though they were two, they experienced a connection greater than their distinctive differences. They truly completed each other in a manner that every marriage should strive for.

Therefore shall a man leave his father and his mother, and shall cleave unto his wife: and they shall be one flesh. And they were both naked, the man and his wife, and were not ashamed. (Genesis 2:24-25)

After they sinned, their view of God, each other and the world would be forever changed. When the Lord approached them, they were no longer comforted but frighten. Fear is always present in the place of uncertainty. Fear builds walls which support and strengthen separation. When the walls of separation are in place, we no longer find the broken relationship as a place of refuge. Isaiah write that sin obscures our view of God.

When the walls of separation are in place, we no longer find the broken relationship as a place of refuge

But your iniquities have separated between you and your God, and your sins have hid his face from you, that he will not hear. Isaiah 59:2

Isaiah speaks of how iniquity and sin impacts our relationship with God. The overall impact is that God will not hear us. How is it possible that God who hears everything would not hear us? Paul answers this in Romans 10 this way:

How then shall they call on him in whom they have not believed? And how shall the believe in him of whom they have not heard? And How shall they hear without a preacher? Romans 10:14

The inference is that God doesn't hear because people are not calling to him. It is the recognition of God's presence that keeps man calling on him. Man's recognition of the existence of God is muted by the separation produced by sin. Sin's power is broken when the God is visible in the life of man.

Man's recognition of the existence of God is muted by the separation produced by sin.

Because of sin, Adam and his wife were no longer comforted by the presence of God. They sought refuge by covering themselves with fig leaves. Fig leaves suggest a confidence in what God had created instead of God. Paul warns us of this propensity in carnal man to place things created in a place above the creator.

Sin also effected the relationship between man and his wife. Now the relationship designed by God to be complimentary would now be complicated.

Sin so stretched the fabric of the marriage relationship that Adam view of his wife would change from "you are flesh of my flesh; bone of my bone and you were taken from me" to "your name shall be called Eve." Her new identify formed a new connection based upon a function. She was the mother of all living. The shifted from being Adam's companion to the mother of the world.

The Paradigm of Separation

In creation, God used this paradigm, dividing then light from darkness, the firmament of heaven and the gathering of the water in one place to make room for dry land. He even made everything he created with a distinctive make-up. This was a created incompatibility with other species of animals. In creation you see the terms divide gather together, after his kind as terms that completely recognizes differences.

These are the generations of the heavens and of the earth when they were created, in the day that the Lord God made the earth and the heavens, And every plant of the field before it was in the earth, and every herb of the field before it grew: for the Lord God had not caused it to rain upon the earth, and there was not a man to till the ground. (Genesis 2:4-5)

The paradigm of separation brought order to a dark an empty place.

The text describes God's good old days as a time when everything functioned according to its design. It was good. The paradigm of separation brought order to a dark an empty place. The order of creation always intrigued me. It started with the basic and moved to the more complex. A foundation was laid for each thing created by that which preceded it. Light came out of darkness. Out of the water came dry land. Out of the land came animals, trees and vegetation. From the ocean fish and birds.

The animals created only had one purpose to roam the earth. The beauty that they provided pleased God. He called the creation of them good. The same was true of the grass and tree. God gave clear assignments to the more complex things in creation by providing purpose to their existence. Though light existed before the sun and moon, God shifted the responsibility to bring light to the earth to them once they were created. God was the source of life for all he created. Then he gave vegetation an assignment to be the earthly source of nourishment for all living things. The earth remained undisturbed by storms or rain.

Then God created man. Though formed from the ground, his real nature was acquired from his unique relationship to God. Man was not the only being that came from the earth. In fact, all of the land-based animals came from the earth, and life was in them. Man was made in the image of God. He was made to be like Him in complexity and authority. It was only after God breathed into him the breath of life that man became a living soul.

> All things in the world are sensitive to the mantle of authority that the Lord has placed on them.

Mankind, being the most complex of God's creation, assignment would be different from all that was created. The DNA of God was his makeup. He would be a mirror to all that was in the earth of God's authority. All things in the world are sensitive to the mantle of authority that the Lord has placed on them.

Sin corrupted the identity of man. Though all of creation longs to see the manifestation of the sons of God. Mankind has masked the true nature of God within them because of the deceitful nature of sin. Our full authority is known by all of creation but is hidden from us. Now we use our distinctiveness as a source of debate, conflict and fear.

Separation was celebrated in the Old Testament. God called men to be separated unto him for a purpose. He would call a people to be His own. Over 613 laws were written to providing a distinction between them and all the world. Even God used this paradigm as a vehicle through which His son would come into the world.

But when the fulness of the time was come, God sent forth his Son, made of a woman, made under the law, To redeem them that were under the law, that we might receive the adoption of sons. (Galatians 4:4-5)

Jesus was born during this paradigm of separation. He was born into a covenant family. He went through the same challenges that men face. He also adhered to the covenant of the Jewish people, being a Jew himself. Yet his purpose was to save the world. His plan would go beyond the boundaries of the nation of Israel and touch everyone that would hear. The Lord told Abraham:

That in blessing I will bless thee, and in multiplying I will multiply thy seed as the stars of the heaven, and as the sand which is upon the sea shore; and thy seed shall possess the gate of his enemies; And in thy seed shall all the nations of the earth be blessed; because thou hast obeyed my voice. (Genesis 22:17-18)

> Though Jesus was born a Jew, His purpose was to save the world.

The promise that God spoke to Abraham would take nothing less than a miracle to com to pass. He and his wife had no children of their own and they were well past the child bearing years. Yet the Lord said that that He would have the privilege of enjoying fatherhood, which was highly cherished in those days. To confirm his promise God had done a radical thing. He changed his name. Growing up he would go by the name Abram. That name meant high Father. As he grew in matured into a man, he would, as customary in those days take a wife with the hopes of starting a family. After years went by, he and his wife begin to realize that children were not apart of there future together. This had become their reality and they seem to be ok with it. But something amazing happened. They received a visitation from heaven declaring that he would ended become a father even in his old age. The words sparked enough hope that again Abram begin to believe that it was possible. Sarai, his wife even offered here handmaiden thinking that maybe she was the reason they had not had children. Her suspicions proved to be correct. The problem wasn't with her husband. The reality was, she was the reason that they could not have children.

It was on a second visitation that Abram and Sarai's name would be changed as God would confirm that it would be through Sarah that the blessed seed would come. This to demonstrate the paradigm of separation that existed in the old covenant. In the old covenant we are face to

> The new covenant came with a promise that sin's limitation would not be a barrier to the promise of God.

face with the reality of sin's effect on our life, bringing with it, death. The new covenant came with a promise that sin's limitation would not be a barrier to the promise of God. The new covenant would bring with it, life.

The thief cometh not, but for to steal, and to kill, and to destroy: I am come that they might have life, and that they might have it more abundantly. (John 10:10)

The source of life is the words that comes from the mouth of God. Because God is speaking to us life is possible. Sin prevents us from hearing what the Lord is saying to us and limits our faith.

For unto us was the gospel preached, as well as unto them: but the word preached did not profit them, not being mixed with faith in them that heard it. (Hebrews 4:2)

The missing element was not the word of God. It was preached. However, if there are no hearers to be impacted by that word faith will not arise. The effectiveness of the preaching of God's word relies on a deposit of faith. Faith comes with the word of God, however only those that receive the word have access to the faith that empowers it.

The Church: Conformational or Transformational

2 And be not conformed to this world: but be ye transformed by the renewing of your mind, that ye may prove what is that good, and acceptable, and perfect, will of God (Romans 12:2)

What does the culture of believers look like? Is it necessary for a culture to change in order to be Christian? These questions form the core to the mission of the believer in its pursuit of the great commission. The western believer develops a view or perception of what the community of believers should look like. Unfortunately, the world is much bigger than our unique experience. It is into the world that the great commission sends the disciples of Jesus Christ. Just as we have a point of view from which we minister, so did the early disciples. They were Jewish by birth. That distinction came with a long history of

> Though the introduction of sin into the world tarnish what God intended man to be, it did not take away the desire mankind to be like him.

tradition that could not be completely ignored. They had to develop healthy perspective of their history, culture as it related to their faith in Christ. The internal conflict must have been quite a challenge, yet it seems that they made the adjustment well. They did not do it by abandoning their history or culture. They saw all that they had learned as foundational to the newfound revelation found in Christ alone. This did not change their culture or history, it built upon it. Paul speaks of us as wise master builders in that we watch carefully how we build on the foundation.

In Genesis we see two major building projects. Both projects were massive in scope. Both projects would have a capacity to accommodate the masses. One project would be God designed, the other would be man oriented. One would provide salvation, the other identification. How important is a name. The Ecclesiastes 7:1 would declare "A good name is better than precious ointment...". But should a good name be our pursuit?

Genesis 6:13-22 The ark was designed by God to save mankind from the evil that pervaded the society. Man always finds a way to mock or undermined plans with a source other than their own imagination.

Genesis 11:4 They said "let us build ourselves a city,... and let us make a name for ourselves."

It was their design and for their purpose. Notice it was for them to make a name for themselves. Today, we must be aware of this mindset. It is a mindset based in pride. It is a celebration of self. Though their plan was to build a tower to reach God, their objective was to bring themselves to a place with God. Since the fall of Adam man has been on a journey to the image of God. In creation God makes a declarative statement to make man in his own image. God declare man to be like him. Though the introduction of sin into the world tarnish what God intended man to be, it did not take away the desire mankind to be like him. Satan capitalized on that desire with Eve with a promise that sought a pathway to God likeness through disobedience and rebellion.

Isaiah 14:13-14 You said in your heart, I will ascend to heaven; above the stars of God I will set my throne on high...

Satan always has a plan the is different from God's plan. His purpose is to replaces God's ideas with his own. While his goal is to take the throne of your heart for himself, he is completely satisfied with allowing us to take the throne. He recognizes that there is only room for one on the heart's throne. The only thing of importance to him is that God does not occupy the thrown of the heart. Anything other than God is a win in his mind. His overall intent is to remove God from the center of man's life and replace God with a substituted. These substitutes come in many forms.

Satan's goal is to move God's rule? What shall our response be. We must accept a new paradigm. The paradigm of separation will always be inconsistent with the overall will of God. His message of love is not limited by our ideals or standard. We must no longer be guided by history culture or even denominational identity. As children of God we must not allow the labels of men to guide our activity. We are sons and daughters of the living God. It is His Spirit that guides us.

The great commission given to us to go into all the world has and continues to change the lives of those that hear and receive it. We must never underestimate the gospels impact on those that carry it. The more you share with others, the more God shares with you. Carry the message. Respond to the word and go. The greatest disciple that is made, the greatest witness that comes forth in the process will be its impact upon you. To fine our true destiny we really have no choice but to answer God's call to go.

Isaiah 55:5 (KJV 1900): 5 Behold, thou shalt call a nation that thou knowest not, And nations that knew not thee shall run unto the Because of the Lord thy God, And for the Holy One of Israel; for he hath glorified thee.

Printed and bound by PG in the USA

USA2019PG1L